Hector Parrot and the Great Cake Robbery

Written and illustrated by Ed Eaves

Collins

Meet Hector Parrot, schoolboy detective. As Hector likes to say …

"A mystery a day, that's my way!"

For fun, Hector is a hardworking pupil at Clever Clogs Academy. And for even more fun, Hector works hard catching criminals!

All over Bigtown a mysterious masked thief is swiping cakes and pinching sweet treats.

Mmm, I've been sooo looking forward to my …

Oi, that's my cream horn!

Ooh, what a lovely …

Hey, my tasty pastry!

Inspector Yapp, Bigtown Police's finest officer, is baffled and bamboozled. There's only one boy for the job.

Two days later.

Ladies, gentlemen, boys, girls and, err, dogs? Welcome to the final of the Bigtown Baking Competition!

A big round of applause for the wonderful finalists, Bella Fondant, Sally Sprinkles and Sammy Self-Raising!

Later.

And now, the mayor will announce the winner of the Bigtown Baking Competition!

It looks like the thief didn't show up after all.

That's a relief!

Hmm.

Oh, what a delicious day we've had! The winner of the Bigtown Baking Competition is ... Bella ...

I'm not so sure, Parrot, she looks very sneaky to me. What are you hiding, young lady?

It's, erm, just a … carrot.

A CARROT! The winner of the Bigtown Baking Competition eating a raw carrot?

The Bigtown Baking Competition tent? We're right back where we started. That dog is useless!

Ohhh, now we'll never find the thief. I'm going to be in big trouble with the Chief!

I wouldn't be so sure about that, Inspector.

"Allow me to explain."

"While you have all been enjoying a lovely stroll with this good boy … there's a good boy! Such a good boy!"

"Erm, Hector?"

Ideas for reading

Written by Gill Matthews
Primary Literacy Consultant

Reading objectives:
- discuss and clarify the meanings of words, linking new meanings to known vocabulary
- answer and ask questions
- predict what might happen on the basis of what has been read so far

Spoken language objectives:
- use spoken language to develop understanding through speculating, hypothesising, imagining and exploring ideas
- participate in discussions, presentations, performances, role play, improvisations and debates

Curriculum links: Relationships education: Respectful relationships, Art
Interest words: mysterious, baffled, bamboozled, panicking
Word count: 681

Build a context for reading

- Ask children to look at the front cover of the book and to read the title.
- Discuss what they think the book is going to be about.
- Explore why they think someone would steal a cake.
- Read the back cover blurb.
- Point out that this is a graphic novel. Explore what they know about graphic novels. If necessary, explain that in graphic novels, the story is told mainly through pictures and speech.

Understand and apply reading strategies

- Ask children to turn to pp2–3.
- Discuss what they notice about the layout of these pages. Ask them to identify the order in which the boxes should be read.
- Explore children's understanding of speech bubbles by asking them to point to the speech bubbles on these pages and the text boxes.